To Dr. M. Jerry Weiss

—W.D.M.

To Etta Taylor

—L.J.

Amistad is an imprint of HarperCollins Publishers.

The art for this book was created using acrylic, pastel, and spray paint layered on museum board.

The author would like to acknowledge the following sources: *The Autobiography of Malcolm X*, by Malcolm X, with the assistance of Alex Haley, Ballantine Books, 1992; *Malcolm X: His Life and Legacy*, by Kevin Brown, The Millbrook Press, 1995; various recorded speeches of Malcolm X

Malcolm X · Text copyright © 2000 by Walter Dean Myers · Illustrations copyright © 2000 by Leonard Jenkins
Manufactured in China by South China Printing Company Ltd. All rights reserved. www.harperchildrens.com

Library of Congress Cataloging-in-Publication Data
Myers, Walter Dean, 1937–
   Malcolm X : a fire burning brightly / by Walter Dean Myers ; illustrated by Leonard Jenkins.
      p.   cm.
   ISBN 0-06-027707-6. — ISBN 0-06-027708-4 (lib. bdg.) — ISBN 0-06-056201-3 (pbk.)
   1. X, Malcolm, 1925–1965—Juvenile literature.   2. Black Muslims—Biography—Juvenile literature.
I. Jenkins, Leonard.   II. Title.
BP223.Z8L5765   2000   99-21527
320.54'092—dc21   CIP
[B]

Typography by Matt Adamec   ❖

MALCOLM X
A FIRE BURNING BRIGHTLY

BY WALTER DEAN MYERS
ILLUSTRATED BY LEONARD JENKINS

Amistad

HARPERCOLLINS*PUBLISHERS*

"WHOEVER HEARD OF A REVOLUTION WHERE THEY LOCK ARMS AND SING 'WE SHALL OVERCOME'? YOU DON'T DO THAT IN A REVOLUTION! YOU DON'T DO ANY SINGING BECAUSE YOU'RE TOO BUSY SWINGING!"

"YOU DON'T HAVE A PEACEFUL REVOLUTION. YOU DON'T HAVE A TURN THE CHEEK REVOLUTION. THERE'S NO SUCH THING AS A NONVIOLENT REVOLUTION!"

The man talking was Malcolm X. The audience responded with applause and nervous laughter. They believed in this brother, even though they knew that what he was saying was dangerous. Some said that the police were recording everything Malcolm said. Malcolm knew it was true, but he hadn't come this far to turn back or soften his message about winning freedom, justice, and equality for blacks in America.

Where he had come from was a small black community in Omaha, Nebraska. He wasn't Malcolm X then but Malcolm Little, the son of Elder Earl Little and his wife, Louise. Malcolm's earliest memories were of watching his father speak before black audiences in Omaha. Besides being a preacher, his father was also president of the local chapter of the Universal Negro Improvement Association (U.N.I.A.), an organization that urged black people to improve themselves by starting their own businesses and educating themselves.

But jobs were scarce in Omaha, especially for blacks, and the family moved to East Lansing, Michigan, when Malcolm was four.

Young Malcolm admired his father very much, but it was from his mother that he received his love of learning. Louise Little loved to read and spent hours teaching Malcolm and his brothers and sisters how to read and do arithmetic.

"UP, YOU MIGHTY RACE, YOU CAN ACCOMPLISH WHAT YOU WILL!"

Malcolm's father knew that if his children were going to do well, they would have to be good students. They would have to understand their own history. As he struggled to feed and clothe his growing family, he also worked hard to give them a sense of pride, both in themselves and in their race. There were constant threats from people who did not like his talking about supporting black businesses and having black pride.

Early one morning in September 1931, the police arrived at the Little house with news that Elder Little had been killed in an accident. He had been found crushed to death under a trolley. Louise Little and her children were devastated. Rumors around town reported that Malcolm's father had been killed by people who didn't like what he had been saying about blacks needing to stand up for their rights.

With her husband gone and few jobs available for black women, Louise Little had a difficult time making ends meet. Malcolm often went to school hungry. As things worsened at home, Malcolm's mother became so ill, she could no longer support the family. Social workers split up the children, placing Malcolm, his younger brothers, and a sister in different foster homes. When Malcolm started playing pranks in class, he was sent to a detention home.

Despite the family's troubles, Malcolm kept up his grades and was popular with the other students. He played for the school basketball team and was elected class president in seventh grade. He remembered his father telling him that he could make something of himself. In his heart he knew that his father had been right. Malcolm knew that he was bright, and that he should be able to use his intelligence to make a living.

When Malcolm was in junior high school, a conversation with his English teacher had a profound impact on him. His teacher asked him what he wanted to be when he grew up. Malcolm proudly told him that he wanted to be a lawyer.

"We all like you," his teacher told him, "you know that." He went on to say that Malcolm should be realistic about being a Negro. "You're good with your hands. . . . Why don't you plan on carpentry?" he said.

Malcolm felt hurt and discouraged. What good did it do to be a good student at school, and to get along with all the other kids, if he couldn't be what he wanted just because of the color of his skin? Sensing that there was no future for him in Michigan, Malcolm asked his half sister Ella if he could move to her home in Boston, Massachusetts. He left Michigan at the end of the school year.

Boston was an exciting place to fourteen-year-old Malcolm. Young black men wore zoot suits and had their hair straightened. They had their own way of talking and even a cool way of walking. Maybe Malcolm couldn't be a lawyer, but he could do what the sharp guys did in Boston. He had his reddish hair straightened, and he bought himself a powder-blue suit and a wide-brimmed hat.

"Man, you are looking good, just like you should!" his friend Shorty would tell him. Malcolm started feeling good about himself again. He liked belonging to the slick crowd in Boston. He worked a number of jobs, including one as a sandwich seller for the railroad on the train route between Boston and New York.

In New York's Harlem community, Malcolm became fascinated by the night-club life, the parties, and street hustles. "Big Red," as he was now called, moved easily in this new and exciting world. It was as if he had become a different person from the one he had been in Michigan.

**"NEW YORK WAS HEAVEN TO ME.
AND HARLEM WAS SEVENTH HEAVEN!"**

Malcolm took his sharp suits and snappy hats from New York's hot spots to Boston. In Boston, he joined a gang that robbed apartments. But the "slick" life he was leading came to a quick end when his gang was arrested.

Malcolm was twenty-one when he went to prison. He had no one to blame for his troubles but himself, and he knew it. What had happened to the bright boy he had once been? To the teenager who wanted to be a lawyer?

Bitter with his surroundings and with himself, Malcolm spent most of his time in Charlestown State Prison reading. Books had a lot more to offer a young man with a good mind than the convicts he was with did.

"ANYONE WHO HAS READ A GREAT DEAL CAN IMAGINE THE NEW WORLD THAT [READING] OPENED."

Writing to his brothers and sisters was one of the few pleasures Malcolm had in jail besides reading books. One letter from his brother Reginald particularly interested him. Reginald had joined the Nation of Islam, a political and religious organization dedicated to the betterment of black people. The Nation of Islam was headed by the Honorable Elijah Muhammad. Malcolm was so inspired by the teachings of the Black Muslims, as they were also called, that he wrote to Elijah Muhammad. He was thrilled when Elijah Muhammad began corresponding regularly with him.

Elijah Muhammad told Malcolm to consider himself not a prisoner, but a man who was about to make a change for the better in his life. "At the bottom of the social heap is the black man in the big city ghetto. He lives night and day with the rats and cockroaches and drowns himself with alcohol to try and forget where and what he is," Elijah Muhammad said. "But when you get him you've got the best kind of Muslim. He's the most fearless. He will stand the longest." Malcolm was ready to make that change.

In August 1952, when he was paroled from prison, Malcolm Little had become a member of the Nation of Islam.

Having gone from the good student in Omaha to the big-city hustler, Malcolm had now taken on a new identity. Like many Black Muslims, he dropped his family name and took the last name X. He said that represented his lost African name.

The Nation of Islam believed in black people helping themselves, as Malcolm's father had believed, but also in

separating black and white people. Malcolm was a passionate speaker, and he was so successful at recruiting new members that Elijah Muhammad sent him to build up the Nation of Islam mosque in Harlem. It was a natural place for Malcolm to be. He knew the streets; he knew the street life and the language of the people he was seeking to convert. In his own way, Malcolm was following in his father's footsteps. In New York, Malcolm met Sister Betty X. Eventually they would marry and have six daughters.

"THE WHITE MAN *WANTS* BLACK MEN TO STAY IMMORAL, UNCLEAN AND IGNORANT. AS LONG AS WE STAY IN THESE CONDITIONS WE WILL KEEP ON BEGGING HIM AND HE WILL CONTROL US. WE NEVER CAN WIN FREEDOM AND JUSTICE AND EQUALITY UNTIL WE ARE DOING SOMETHING FOR OURSELVES!"

During the 1950s, Malcolm X could often be seen speaking on street corners in Harlem. This was a turbulent time in America. In 1954, the Supreme Court ruled in *Brown v. Board of Education* that segregation in schools was wrong. This ruling helped fuel the civil rights movement, which worked toward securing equal rights for black Americans.

The leaders in the movement had different ideas about how to accomplish their goals. One group believed that black people should appeal to Americans for equal rights and demonstrate their determination to get those rights by peaceful protests. It supported moderate, well-educated men such as the Reverend Martin Luther King, Jr., who preached nonviolence, for positions of leadership. But it seemed to ignore the kind of urban street people to whom Malcolm X appealed. Other groups in the civil rights movement, such as the Nation of Islam, believed that black people should *demand* equal rights, and be willing to fight for them if necessary.

Malcolm was a fiery speaker with a growing following. As the civil rights movement grew larger and larger, Malcolm began making a name for himself at home and abroad with the intention of seeking greater publicity for the Nation of Islam.

Malcolm preached that black men should not drink, smoke, use drugs, steal, or commit other crimes. He used his own story to show how he had turned his life around. Malcolm also preached that black people should separate from whites. Malcolm was labeled a bigot and a troublemaker by some white and black people. Even more alarming to some people was Malcolm's rejection of nonviolence. Malcolm preached that blacks should demand justice "using arms if necessary." Elijah Muhammad began to feel that Malcolm's outspokenness was making the Nation of Islam look bad.

"YOU DON'T HAVE A PEACEFUL REVOLUTION."

As violence against blacks increased in the 1960s, Malcolm's speeches became more heated. Although Malcolm was enormously popular, Elijah Muhammad told him that he needed permission before he could issue any more public statements. A rift was growing between Elijah Muhammad and his most popular minister. Malcolm was frustrated, because he felt that the Nation of Islam's policy of noninvolvement wasn't in keeping with the times. Malcolm, who had changed so much in his life, was about to make one more change.

In March 1964, Malcolm announced that he was leaving the Nation of Islam. He wanted to start a new organization that would include black men of all religions and that would be an even more active force for change. Two months later, Malcolm made a religious pilgrimage to Mecca, the holiest city in the Islamic religion.

In Mecca, Malcolm experienced a sense of unity with the other pilgrims, who were of all colors. For the first time, Malcolm's outlook no longer included rejecting others because of their color. "True Islam doesn't have room for racism," he said, "because people of all colors and races who accept its religious principles can accept each other as brothers and sisters."

Malcolm's new flexibility pleased a lot of moderates in the black community. More and more people were looking for new leadership in the battle for civil rights. By no longer rejecting people because of their color, Malcolm and his message had become much more acceptable. Others felt they no longer knew what Malcolm stood for. The break with the Nation of Islam had not been healed.

On a cold day in February 1965, at the age of 39, Malcolm was giving a speech in Harlem's Audubon Ballroom. The speech had just started when suddenly gunfire erupted. There were wild moments of confusion as people ran toward the exits. But one thing was soon clear. Malcolm X lay dying on the floor. Three members of the Nation of Islam were later convicted of his murder.

Malcolm X was a complex man living in a complex time of turmoil and change. He had blazed his way through the history of the fifties and sixties in America. And like so many flames, he warmed many with his leadership and insight. Others he burned with his opposition and scorn. And like flames that burn too brightly, his light was too soon extinguished.

"TO COME RIGHT DOWN TO IT, IF I TAKE THE KIND OF THINGS IN WHICH I BELIEVE, THEN ADD TO THAT THE KIND OF TEMPERAMENT THAT I HAVE, PLUS THE ONE HUNDRED PER CENT DEDICATION I HAVE TO WHATEVER I BELIEVE IN—THESE ARE INGREDIENTS WHICH MAKE IT JUST ABOUT IMPOSSIBLE FOR ME TO DIE OF OLD AGE."

CHRONOLOGY

1925   **Malcolm grows up listening to his father preach.**

"Up, you mighty race, you can accomplish what you will!"
—Reverend Earl Little

1931   **Malcolm's father dies in Lansing, Michigan.**

"The image of him that made me proudest was his campaigning with the words of Marcus Garvey."

1938–1941   **Malcolm faces difficult times in his childhood.**

"We children watched our anchor giving way."

1941   **Malcolm moves to Boston to live with his half sister Ella.**

"One statue in the Boston Commons astonished me: a Negro named Crispus Attucks, who had been the first man to fall in the Boston Massacre. I had never known anything like that."

1943–1946   **Malcolm becomes a hustler in Harlem, New York.**

"New York was heaven to me. And Harlem was Seventh Heaven!"

"I was a true hustler—uneducated, unskilled at anything honorable, and I considered myself nervy and cunning enough to live by my wits, exploiting any prey that presented itself."

1946   **Malcolm is arrested and sentenced to ten years in prison.**

"I had gotten to the point where I was walking on my own coffin. It's a law of the rackets that every criminal expects to get caught."

1947–1952   **In prison, Malcolm becomes an avid reader and converts to Islam.**

"In prison I found Allah and the religion of Islam and it completely transformed my life."

"Anyone who has read a great deal can imagine the new world that [reading] opened."

"My alma mater was books, a good library."

1952   **Malcolm hears Elijah Muhammad speak.**

"Elijah spoke of how the black man was kidnapped from his homeland and stripped of his language, his culture, his family structure, his family name, until the black man in America did not even realize who he was."

1954   **Malcolm becomes a minister of New York Temple Number Seven.**

"We didn't land on Plymouth Rock, my brothers and sisters—Plymouth Rock landed on us!"

"The white man *wants* black men to stay immoral, unclean and ignorant. As long as we stay in these conditions we will keep on begging him and he will control us. We never can win freedom and justice and equality until we are doing something for ourselves!"

"My black brothers and sisters—*no* one will know *who* we are . . . until we know who we are! We never will be able to *go* anywhere until we know *where* we are!"

"Whoever heard of a revolution where they lock arms and sing 'we shall overcome'? You don't do that in a revolution! You don't do any singing because you're too busy swinging!"

"You don't have a peaceful revolution. You don't have a turn the cheek revolution. There's no such thing as a nonviolent revolution!"

"Yes, I am an extremist. The black race . . . is in extremely bad condition."

1958   **Malcolm X marries Sister Betty X on January 14.**

"I love Betty. She's the only woman I ever even thought about loving."

1964   **Malcolm breaks with the Nation of Islam and goes to Mecca.**

"The holiest and most sacred city on earth. The fountain of truth, love, peace, and brotherhood."

"There were tens of thousands of pilgrims, from all over the world. They were of all colors, from blue-eyed blonds to black-skinned Africans. But we were all participating in the same ritual, displaying a spirit of unity and brotherhood that my experiences in America had led me to believe never could exist between the white and the non-white."

"I'm for truth, no matter who tells it. I'm for justice, no matter who it is for or against."

"I believe in recognizing every human being as a human being—neither white, black, brown, or red."

"True Islam doesn't have room for racism because people of all colors and races who accept its religious principles can accept each other as brothers and sisters."

1965   **Malcolm X is assassinated in Harlem.**

"To come right down to it, if I take the kind of things in which I believe, then add to that the kind of temperament that I have, plus the one hundred per cent dedication I have to whatever I believe in—these are ingredients which make it just about impossible for me to die of old age."